Contents

The Meditator's Nest
Vol. 2

A MAHAYANA
MEDITATION MANUAL

VAJRA
BOOKS

Published & Distributed by
Vajra Books
Jyatha, Thamel, P.O. Box 21779, Kathmandu, Nepal
Tel.: 977-1-4220562, Fax: 977-1-4246536
e-mail: bidur_la@mos.com.np
www.vajrabooks.com.np

ISBN 978-9937-623-61-2

Printed in Nepal

Preface

We are delighted to publish a meditation manual this year inspired by the teachings of Khenpo Jamyang Tenzin at the International Buddhist Academy in Kathmandu.

In June 2011 Khenpo-la offered a month-long series of teachings entitled "The Meditator's Nest" based on the Mahayana pith instructions from the Lamdré tradition. During that month Khenpo-la led daily guided meditations extracted from *The Beautiful Ornament of the Three Visions* (also known simply as *The Three Visions*) by Ngorchen Könchog Lhundrup. The meditations in the present manual are based on this text and are prefaced by introductions to provide some context for each practice. In this way they form a comprehensive guide for practitioners, from the practice of going for refuge up to the cultivation of superior insight.

Khenpo-la's teachings from 2011 have also been transcribed and are being published under the title *The Meditator's Nest: Building a Spiritual Practice*; it is an invaluable companion to this volume.

This manual was prepared by Christian Bernert under the guidance of Khenpo Jamyang Tenzin. We would like to thank Vivian Paganuzzi and Steven Rhodes for kindly editing the entire text, Cristina Vanza for designing the cover and helping with the layout, and everyone who contributed with suggestions and advice. We also thank Claire Pullinger for the beautiful photograph of the statue of Buddha

Shakyamuni from Bodhgaya, and Ven. Rinchen Gyaltsen for the blue flower. The stanzas from the *Lalitavistara Sutra*, the *Sutra of Instructions to the King* and the *Introduction to the Middle Way* are taken from Adam Pearcey, *A Compendium of Quotations* (2008). The verses from *The Way of the Bodhisattva* (chapters 2 and 8) are taken from Shantideva, *The Way of the Bodhisattva* (2006).

Chödung Karmo Translation Group
International Buddhist Academy, Kathmandu
February 2016

Foreword

The innumerable teachings of Lord Buddha ultimately all serve a single purpose: to free the mind of mental afflictions and of anything that would obscure or distort our vision of reality. For the sake of followers genuinely interested in the practice the masters have condensed these teachings into pith instructions, providing clear advice on the essential points of practice. Over the centuries many individuals have achieved the highest levels of realization and freedom through practice based on such authentic instructions, and if we put these instructions into practice, we too will obtain results.

This meditation manual is based on the pith instructions from the famous Sakya teachings known as *Nang Sum*, or *The Three Visions*, which are part of the Lamdré system. In our tradition these instructions are always given before one enters the Vajrayana, and they are meant to be cultivated and mastered, at least to a certain degree, before one engages in serious tantric practice. It may be the case that we have been practicing deity yoga for many years without there being a fundamental change in us. This is probably because we have not worked enough on the foundations of the path, which are precisely the content of this manual.

These instructions will be especially beneficial for those who cannot have regular and close contact with their teachers in order to consult them on the details of their practice. By just following the instructions found herein, significant progress can be made. All it needs is sincere interest, consistency, diligence, and patience in one's practice, and most of all the courage to honestly look into ourselves.

To supplement the brief instructions in this book I advise you to consult the translation of *The Beautiful Ornament of the Three Visions* by Ngorchen Könchog Lhundrup as often as possible.

I wish everyone on this path the best success in their practice.

Khenpo Jamyang Tenzin

International Buddhist Academy, Kathmandu
June 2013

Introduction

This manual is designed to guide anyone interested in Buddhist meditation and mind training through some of the most important steps of the practice. It can be used as an introduction to Mahayana Buddhist meditation as it is presented in the Tibetan tradition, as well as a manual for daily practice covering the fundamentals, from the practice of taking refuge to the higher practices of bodhicitta.

The meditations presented in this manual are inspired by and to a great extent based on the practices taught in *The Three Visions* (*Nang Sum*) by Ngorchen Könchog Lhundrup and arranged according to the sequence given in the instructions on *Parting from the Four Attachments*, the famous teaching on mind training from the Sakya tradition.

The manual is composed of four sets of practices, corresponding to the four stages of the path: refuge, renunciation, compassion, and wisdom. The initial stage, called "Taking a safe direction in life," consists in building up one's confidence and trust in the Three Precious Jewels. The second stage, "Setting priorities: turning towards the Dharma," is composed of four contemplations designed to bring about a fundamental change in one's outlook on life. In the third stage, "A change of heart: for the benefit of all," one cultivates the states of mind that will help one transcend self-centered ambitions, and in the last, "Learning to see," one learns to cultivate the highest levels of Mahayana meditation, calm abiding and superior insight.

In order to understand the theory behind the practices presented here we advise the reader to refer to *The Meditator's Nest: Building a Spiritual Practice* by Khenpo Jamyang Tenzin, which is a companion volume to this manual, and to *The Beautiful Ornament of the Three Visions* by Ngorchen Könchog Lhundrup, from which the meditations are extracted. We also advise readers to consult *The Three Levels of Spiritual Perception* by Deshung Rinpoche (which is an excellent oral commentary to *The Three Visions*), *Parting from the Four Attachments* by Chogyé Trichen Rinpoche, and the *Teachings on Sakya Pandita's* Clarifying the Sage's Intent by Khenchen Appey Rinpoche. Please refer to the bibliography at the end of this manual.

The structure of each session

Each meditation session follows the same basic structure:

1. Opening section
2. Main practice
3. Closing section

1. The opening section

- First of all, create an environment conducive for the training by **relaxing the body and the mind**.

- Then **check your motivation** for the practice: why are you doing this?

- To bring your meditation into alignment with the path of liberation taught by the Buddha, give it the right orientation by **going for refuge** to the Three Precious Jewels, followed by a short silent meditation. (This practice forms the first chapter of this book.)

  Note: The practice of going for refuge can also become a main practice, in which case the refuge formula is repeated many times to deepen and stabilize the corresponding mental state.

- At an advanced stage of practice (from chapter 9 onwards) the **generation of bodhicitta** becomes an integral part of the opening section. However, practitioners familiar with the cultivation of this state, as well as those naturally inclined to generate this altruistic intention, may include it in the opening section of their practice from the very outset of their training. In this way whatever state of mind one cultivates thereafter will become a Mahayana practice.

2. **The main practices** change over time, but all serve the single purpose of **reducing and eventually eliminating mental afflictions and ignorance.** Traditionally, one begins by developing a stable refuge practice as a foundation for the path. Then one cultivates a sequence of specific states of mind that will enable one to turn on the inner engine, so to speak, and make steady progress.

This manual contains twelve meditations, each building on the previous one. The longer ones are divided into several sections, and you can spend as much time as you want on each section. Any one of them could constitute your entire practice for weeks, or even months, at a time.

3. **The closing section** is the practice of **dedicating the positive potential** generated through one's mind training towards the liberation of all beings without exception.

After the meditation

Formal meditation is the most effective tool to cultivate wholesome mental states and habits, but it is not an end in itself. To ensure steady progress on the path there needs to be continuity in one's practice in between the sessions as well. To this end it is essential to cultivate mindfulness and introspection in daily life, adopting a conduct in harmony with the teachings to support one's development. It is also recommended to frequently reflect on the topics contemplated during the meditation sessions. In this way the time spent on the cushion will support one's daily life, and one's daily life will support the formal meditation practice.

Getting started: sit and relax

It is important not to rush into or out of our meditation practice. By making a "nest" for our practice we are establishing an environment conducive for our spiritual growth. This growth is a natural process which takes time, but it will eventually enable us to let go of our negative habits and conditionings, and thus go beyond what we now call our "comfort zone."

We should begin each session by finding some rest and taking a break from our daily life.

1. Sit upright on a meditation cushion or a chair. Find a posture that will allow you to relax and remain wakeful at the same time. The key points for the body are to have a stable position that will allow you to remain immobile for the duration of the meditation; to keep a straight back; and to relax in the upright posture. (For more detailed instructions on the posture please refer to chapter 11.)

2. Take a few moments to scan the body, from bottom to top and from top to bottom. Note any unnecessary tension and try to relax a bit more with each exhalation. Appreciate fully this opportunity to tune in to the reality of your bodily experience here and now. Take a few minutes for this process.

3. Once you have established some physical ease, bring your attention to the breath and simply observe its natural in- and outflow without controlling or

manipulating it in any way. Stay with your breath, relaxed and wakeful, and count twenty-one cycles of inhalation and exhalation, or stay with it for a few minutes.

4.   With your mind relaxed and focused, reflect on your motivation: what draws you to the practice? If necessary, adjust your motivation to bring it in line with the path to liberation.

5.   Now, start with the formal practice.

Note: The text portions in roman script are the recitations and contemplations meant to be read out loud.

STAGE ONE

Taking a safe direction in life

1. Confidence and trust: going for refuge

Regarded as the entrance to the path of liberation, going for refuge is traditionally done before every Buddhist practice. By actively generating trust in and devotion to the objects of refuge—the Three Precious Jewels (Buddha, Dharma, and Sangha)—one gives whatever practice one cultivates afterwards a very specific direction. Each practice thus becomes a means to achieve true freedom by following the path laid out by the Buddha and validated by his disciples.

At first, the repetition of the refuge prayers may seem artificial, but the words will be filled with meaning as our understanding gradually evolves and deepens through study, contemplation, and meditation. In our daily life we seek refuge in a multitude of objects to gain some sense of security. Such objects may be our relationships, our jobs, food, and even entertainment and distraction. But ultimately these objects are not reliable. By taking refuge in the Buddha we resolve to take the state of awakening, free of confusion, as our ultimate guide in life. By taking refuge in the Dharma we make the conscious decision to follow a wholesome way of living that will allow us to see things as they really are. By taking refuge in the Sangha we resolve to seek the support of others who also follow this path, and who have experienced its benefits, rather than seeking the company of those more confused than ourselves.

Praying for their blessings is a method for ourselves to become open to the wholesome and transformative influence that the Buddha, the Dharma, and the Sangha can have on our lives. They have the ability and power to show us various ways to skillfully relate to our experience, to stop producing causes for our own and others' suffering, and ultimately to attain real freedom. In this way we are not praying to an omnipotent savior whose grace we require for protection. Our prayers are an acknowledgment of the qualities of the Three Precious Jewels, of our need for their support, and also of our own potential to achieve the highest good.

When used as one's main practice, the refuge prayer is repeated as many times as possible. When used to open the other practices laid out later in this manual, the refuge prayer can be recited three, seven, or twenty-one times before proceeding to the main practice.

Visualization

Clearly visualize Buddha Shakyamuni in the space in front of you. He is seated in the full cross-legged posture on a lotus flower and a moon disc, which are on a jewelled throne. His body is of a radiant golden color, he wears the Dharma robes, and his peaceful presence emanates great wisdom and compassion. Behind him is a stack of Dharma scriptures symbolizing the Dharma, and he is surrounded by countless bodhisattvas forming the noble Sangha community.

Imagine that you are going for refuge together with all sentient beings: your mother to your left, father to your right, beings in need of special help and those perceived as enemies in front of you, and all other beings in human form surrounding you.

Consider briefly the fearful suffering resulting from unwholesome deeds, think of the sublime qualities of the Three Precious Jewels, and generate great compassion for all beings in samsara. With one-pointed focus direct your mind to the objects of refuge and recite the **homage prayer**:

> To you, endowed with great compassion for all beings,
> Who wish all beings to find true happiness and be free of suffering,

Who wish those possessing happiness not to be
parted from it,
Who intend to benefit and bring happiness to all
beings,
To you we bow down in reverence.

*Then proceed by **going for refuge**:*

I and all sentient beings throughout endless space
take refuge from this time forth until enlightenment
is reached.

Respectfully with body and speech, and a mind filled
with devotion, we take refuge in the Buddha, the
awakened teacher, perfect in realization and freedom
from obscuration.

Respectfully with body and speech, and a mind filled
with devotion, we take refuge in the holy Dharma,
the essence of the transmitted teachings and of the
realizations and cessations.

Respectfully with body and speech, and a mind filled
with devotion, we take refuge in the noble Sangha,
the Buddha's heirs who uphold the holy Dharma.

(Recite this as many times as possible—at least twenty-one times.)

*After this, pray to the Three Precious Jewels, requesting their
blessings (recite three times):*

We pay homage and take refuge in the Three Precious
Jewels.

We beseech you,
please bless the mind stream of each and every one of us.

Grant your blessings,
so that our minds may turn towards the Dharma.

Grant your blessings,
so that our practice may truly become the liberating
path.

Grant your blessings,
so that the errors on the path may be remedied.

Grant your blessings,
for all perception rooted in confusion to dawn as
transcendental wisdom.

Grant your blessings,
for all thoughts that go against the Dharma to cease.

Grant your blessings,
so that our hearts be filled with loving-kindness and
compassion.

Grant your blessings,
so that we may perfect the training in the two
bodhicittas.

Grant your blessings,
so that we may swiftly attain enlightenment.

Silent Meditation

After the refuge and beseeching prayers, meditate silently as
follows. With a mind filled with trust and admiration think of the
Three Jewels:

In their profound wisdom the Awakened Ones perfectly
understand our condition.

In their limitless compassion they deeply care for us.

They look after us with their enlightened activities.

They protect and bless us with their ability and power,
leading us skillfully along the path to liberation.

*Then train in keeping your mind undistracted in a state of trust
in and pure admiration for the Three Jewels. If any unrelated
thoughts arise during this silent meditation, mentally recite the
above lines again to bring up genuine trust and devotion, and
again try to keep your mind in that state. Repeat this process two
or three times during each session.*

To conclude, **dedicate your merit** *towards the liberation of all
beings:*

> By this merit may I attain omniscience.
> Defeating the foe, the harmful afflictions,
> May I liberate beings from the ocean of samsara,
> Disturbed by the waves of birth, old age, sickness,
> and death.

> Just like the heroic Manjushri,
> Who knows things just as they are,
> And like Samantabhadra too,
> May I follow them all in the ways they have trained,
> And completely dedicate all these virtues.

STAGE TWO

Setting priorities:
turning towards the Dharma

2.   Appreciating what we have: the value of a precious human life

Once we have taken refuge in the Three Jewels and decided to follow the path taught by the Buddha, it is very important to prepare ourselves well for this journey. We need to understand the proper sequence of practice in order to make steady progress on the path. The first point is to check our motivation and to question our priorities in life. Without this we run the risk of calling ourselves a Buddhist for many years without there being any true inner development.

Traditionally it is recommended to cultivate four specific contemplations to bring about a fundamental change in one's outlook, to reset one's priorities in order to focus on what really matters. These four are the contemplations on the precious opportunity we now possess to practice the Dharma, on impermanence and death, on the law of karma, and on the faults of samsara.

*The first of these contemplations, on the precious opportunity we have to actually attain real freedom from suffering and its causes, is designed to generate a deep sense of gratitude, joy, and responsibility not to waste this chance. It remedies the attitude of taking things for granted in our life, and to deeply appreciate the opportunities we have. Begin by **going for refuge** by following the previous instructions. After the brief silent meditation you may generate the supreme motivation of **bodhicitta**:*

> In order to liberate all beings from the ocean of samsara I must attain the state of perfect and complete enlightenment. For that purpose I now engage in the following practice.

Then contemplate the following:

Can I really take all of this for granted: this life, this body, this intelligence, this freedom, all the opportunities I have been given? Is it not the greatest fortune of all, this life I have?

I can travel rather freely. No one is really holding me back. No government, no relatives, no friend, no enemy. I am free to go wherever I want, free to do whatever I desire. Does everyone on earth or even in my own country possess this freedom?

My health is good, or at least good enough to allow me to study and practice the Dharma. How long this will last I simply do not know.

Since beginningless time, from one birth to the next, I have been afflicted by so many sufferings. I have been caught in a perpetual cycle of uncontrollable rebirth, subject to all kinds of suffering and stress, never really free. It is said that to cross samsara's ocean of conditioned existence one must rely upon the boat of the precious human life, a life endowed with the freedoms and conducive conditions allowing one to practice the Dharma. Yet, it is said that it is exceedingly difficult to obtain such a human birth. The power of wholesome deeds and pure actions must be incredibly strong for this to happen. I cannot be certain that this will necessarily happen for me next time around.

In his *The Way of the Bodhisattva*, Shantideva states:

> So hard to find the ease and wealth
> Whereby the aims of beings may be gained.
> If now I fail to turn it to my profit,
> How could such a chance be mine again?

Once obtained, I have a wish-fulfilling gem with the potential to bring inconceivable benefits. Free to practice the Dharma and connected to all necessary conditions, liberation and the attainment of perfect buddhahood are actually within my reach. From this perspective this human body is so much more valuable than any other form of life.

The Buddha taught the means to find release from all suffering, dissatisfaction, stress, and conditioning. The Dharma, his path, is still available to me today. Teachers who have studied his teachings, put the Dharma into practice, and realized its fruits are still alive, sharing their knowledge and experience with us. Everything is there for me to make best use of this life, to use it in a deeply meaningful way. Nothing is set in stone. Whatever circumstances may arise, good or bad, I have the freedom to respond wisely, compassionately, or not.

RESOLVE

Grateful for the incredible freedoms and opportunities I have been given, I shall make sure not to waste them, out of respect for myself and for those less fortunate than me. I will prepare myself for future lives as best I can and strive to let go of all the causes of suffering, and ultimately of anything that obstructs true freedom. I shall practice the Dharma wholeheartedly and make the best of the opportunity I now have. May the Three Precious Jewels guide me on this path.

Deeply reflect on the meaning of these words and pray from the depths of your heart to the Three Precious Jewels that it may happen so.

*To conclude, recite the **dedication prayers:***

By this merit may I attain omniscience.
Defeating the foe, the harmful afflictions,
May I liberate beings from the ocean of samsara,
Disturbed by the waves of birth, old age, sickness, and death.

Just like the heroic Manjushri,
Who knows things just as they are,
And like Samantabhadra too,
May I follow them all in the ways they have trained,
And completely dedicate all these virtues.

3. Cultivating a sense of urgency: contemplating impermanence and death

Having generated deep appreciation for the priceless and rare opportunity we now have, the next step is to develop a sense of urgency and to let go of the worldly attachments that hinder our progress.

The first pitfall one is likely to encounter on the path to liberation is engaging in the spiritual practices out of attachment to this life, hoping to gain some material benefits, fame and praise, or even just ordinary, fleeting feelings of happiness and peace from one's activities. Since the outcome of the practice very much depends on the intention, we are advised to remedy such shortsighted motivations, recognizing that this life does not last forever.

This contemplation has three parts: cultivating awareness of the certainty of death; of the uncertainty of the time of death; and that ordinary self-centered actions are of no avail at the time of death. To make this training more effective you can devote separate meditation sessions to each of these sections individually. Train in the first contemplation until the reality of death is clearly present to your mind. Then move on to the second, and so on.

*Begin your practice by **going for refuge** and, if you wish, generate the supreme motivation of **bodhicitta** (recite three times):*

> In order to liberate all beings from the ocean of samsara I must attain the state of perfect and complete enlightenment. For that purpose I now engage in the following practice.

Then proceed with the contemplations on death:

1. Cultivating awareness of the certainty of death

This contemplation comprises reflections on the fact that everyone born must die, and that it is the nature of the body to disintegrate and perish. Contemplate the following:

Everything in the world is changing, moment by moment. Nothing lasts. My body is ageing every day. Do I look the same as I did two years ago? Will I look the same next year? Will I be in good health next year? I do not know. Can I be certain that I will even be alive next year, next month, or tomorrow? In the *Lalitavistara Sutra* the Buddha states:

> This existence of ours is as transient as autumn clouds.
> To watch the birth and death of beings is like looking at the movement of a dance.
> A lifetime is like a flash of lightning in the sky,
> Rushing by, like a torrent down a steep mountain.

There is no one in the past who, having been born, did not die. Nor is there anyone living at present or yet to be born who will not die. Do I expect to somehow escape this inevitable fact of life? Even the Buddha himself and all the great masters of the past manifested their death. How can I suppose that I, who am totally bound by karma and afflictions, will not perish? How could I ever think I will not die?

The way I relate to this body seems to indicate that I believe it to be permanent. I may think there is some lasting essence to it when in fact it is completely insubstantial. It may be burned to ashes, or cast into the water where it will be devoured piece by piece by fish and other creatures. It may be buried underground where it will be eaten by worms, or rot and putrefy, or left at a charnel ground to be eaten by birds and beasts of prey. It's certain that this body will perish and be disposed of in one way or another. The time is bound to come when it will be clear to all that this body of mine is not in the least bit permanent.

If you reflect in this way but awareness of death and impermanence still does not arise, then reflect in the following manner:

At this time I may be free of serious physical or mental disease. Together with my relatives and beloved ones I enjoy all the privileges of a more or less comfortable life day after day. We make provisions as if we'll live for a thousand years, and constantly engage in trivial activities. The thought of my certain death, however, never crosses my mind. There will be a time when all these things will be left behind and the light of this life will be extinguished.

When the time for me to go will come, I will have to leave everything behind. All the possessions I hold so dear, and all my relatives and friends. I cannot take anything with me. I will have to go alone, proceeding to some unknown place.

RESOLVE

Now, having seriously pondered death, I will repeatedly cultivate this thought, so that it will be firmly impressed upon my mind. This will help me strengthen my motivation to practice the Dharma, which leads to the deathless state. May the Three Precious Jewels assist me on this path.

Sincerely reflect and pray in this way.

2. Cultivating awareness of the uncertainty of the time of death

We contemplate the fact that our lifespan is uncertain, that there are infinite causes of death, and that the few conditions that keep us alive may also cause our death. Contemplate in the following way:

Until now I have spent all my years in constant distraction, not realizing that death can come at any moment. I may have some time left to live, but I may just as well die a sudden death today—how would I know? I simply don't.

The causes that can end this life are countless: I may die in a car accident or a plane crash, in an earthquake, a hurricane, or a flood; I may die from a heart disease, a stroke, a severe form of cancer, or from an infectious or a parasitic disease and so on; I may even die falling down the stairs, slipping in the shower, or choking on food. It is so easy to separate body and mind. When the Lord of Death strikes, I am his. There is no place I could flee to that would be free from the countless causes of death, of which any one may end this life. Even the things that keep me alive, like food and water, can cause my death under certain conditions.

What makes me think that I will not meet with such causes sooner rather than later? There is simply no way to know whether I will die some years from now, tomorrow, or today. If I were to die at this point in my life, I would not have accomplished my previous resolve in any way. What will happen to me at the time of death?

RESOLVE

Not knowing when the time of death may come, I will, from this moment on, try my best to cast off worldly activities carried out solely out of attachment to this life. I must practice the holy Dharma that will surely benefit me at the time of death. May the Precious Jewels guide me so that I may continually keep in mind the reality of death.

Think and pray in this way.

3.   Cultivating awareness that ordinary actions are of no avail at the time of death

Death will certainly come to me, but I can't know when. Other than the Dharma, there is no method that will be of real benefit to me at that time. Until now, however, I have been distracted by unnecessary worldly activities—I have been attached to the objectives of this life alone. I believed all these things to be so important, when it all, in fact, turns out to be quite meaningless and shallow. It shows that the reality of death hasn't really penetrated my mind at all.

Dwell intensively on these thoughts and meditate until a disillusion with worldly life is generated, and intense revulsion for samsara and a genuine sense of sadness arise. Further think:

Until now I have only increased my attachment to worldly pursuits. If I do not wholeheartedly practice the holy Dharma, it would be like returning from a treasure island empty-handed. I would be fooling myself alone! How sad. Food, wealth, worldly goods, and reputation will simply be of no use whatsoever at the time of my death. There is no point in my endless craving for these things, running after and protecting them. Since my beloved ones, my friends and relatives, won't be able to truly help at that time, I must let go of my attachment and desperate clinging to them as well.

The only thing that will be of real benefit at the time of death is a mind free of regrets and concerns, a mind full of wholesome qualities and experience, a mind one with the Dharma.

RESOLVE

It is important to practice the sacred Dharma, a path on which I can surely rely at the time of death, and I must do it now. I shall overcome my laziness and stop this habit of procrastinating. I will engage in the path vigorously, as if putting out a fire that is burning my head and clothing. Directing my mind toward the Precious Jewels, I will strive wholeheartedly and devote myself fully to the practice of the Dharma. May the Precious Jewels guide me in this and help me to fulfill my wishes.

In brief:

Today I will be aware of the fleeting nature of my life. I shall do my best to cultivate what really matters. If there is one thing I know for sure, it is that this life will end one day. When, I simply do not know. Not ignoring this simple truth, I shall use my life in a meaningful way, cultivating whatever it is that will be of benefit when the time comes for me to let go of this life, instead of cultivating attachment to it.

Dwell on these thoughts and pray sincerely.

*To conclude, recite the **dedication prayers**:*

By this merit may I attain omniscience.
Defeating the foe, the harmful afflictions,

May I liberate beings from the ocean of samsara,
Disturbed by the waves of birth, old age, sickness,
and death.

Just like the heroic Manjushri,
Who knows things just as they are,
And like Samantabhadra too,
May I follow them all in the ways they have trained,
And completely dedicate all these virtues.

4. Taking responsibility: reflections on karma— actions and their results

The aim of the previous two contemplations on the precious human life and on impermanence was to reset our priorities in life. Once we are determined to pursue a spiritual way of living, the next step is to reflect on how our actions actually condition our experience. Our spiritual path will be effective only if we understand and respect the law of karma, i.e., actions and their results, as our ability to follow this path entirely depends on the strength of the positive potential accumulated by means of wholesome actions. It is this potential of our actions and the tendencies they create that will shape our experience in this as well as future lives.

*As there are four sections to the contemplation of karma, you may focus on only one topic during your session and move on to the next in the following sitting or, if you have more time, contemplate two or more topics each time. Begin the practice with the **opening section** as above. Then proceed with contemplation on karma.*

1.   General reflections on karma: cause and result

In the natural world every phenomenon arises from specific causes and conditions: the blooming of a flower, the birth of a child, climate change. A lemon seed will produce a lemon tree only, never an orange tree. The same principle is at work in the inner world of our subjective experience: my own well-being and happiness, as well as my stress and suffering, are experienced based on specific causes and conditions. There are no exceptions to this. Learning about the function of cause and effect and the workings of my own mind, I shall learn to live in accordance with this natural law.

Nothing happens accidentally or without a cause. Things depend on their corresponding set of causes and conditions, and these causes and conditions have to be complete for the specific phenomenon to manifest. This holds true for everything I experience, within and outside of myself.

In the experience of happiness and suffering, our heart, our mental states, the mental factors active and activating our experience are critical. From the *Dhammapada*:

> The heart goes before everything; things are ruled by the heart, made of the heart. If one speaks or acts with corrupt intention, suffering will follow, just as the wheel of the cart follows the hoof prints of the ox pulling it.

> The heart goes before everything; things are ruled by the heart, made of the heart. If one speaks or acts with pure intention, happiness will follow, just as the wheel of the cart follows the hoof prints of the ox pulling it.

My "heart" is determined by my intentions. This is why I should always question myself: What is it that is driving me?

A heart filled with clinging and aversion, a mind clouded by delusion, can only give rise to unwholesome states of mind, triggering actions which will bring about suffering to others as well as to oneself. A heart freed of unskillful desires and aversion, a mind which appreciates things as they really are, on the other hand, is not creating unnecessary pain. Such a mind, on the contrary, allows one to be at peace and to act appropriately, with wisdom and compassion. This is so important, because it is our volitional actions which will determine the nature of our future experiences. In the *Sutra of Instructions to the King* the Buddha states:

> When his time has come, even a king has to die,
> And neither his friends nor his wealth can follow him.
> So for us—wherever we stay, wherever we go—
> Karma follows us like a shadow.

RESOLVE

Today I will do my best to be mindful of the intentions behind my deeds. As soon as I see unwholesome motives I shall pause, deter the course of my action, or at least alter my intentions as well as I can.

2. Abstaining from unwholesome deeds

At the time of my death none of this life's food, wealth, or property, and none of my dear family and friends, will follow me. At that time all I will take with me is the potential of the wholesome and unwholesome deeds I have done.

Unwholesome deeds are all actions rooted in the three mental poisons of desire, hatred, and the ignorance which consists of not being able to accurately differentiate between wholesome and unwholesome deeds.

The three unwholesome actions of the body are killing,

stealing, and sexual misconduct; the four unwholesome actions of speech are lying, divisive talk, hurtful speech, and idle gossip; and the three unwholesome actions of the mind are coveting, ill will, and wrong views.

Such actions, rooted in negative states of mind, result in the experience of suffering. This is a natural law. Thus, they are the causes which will bring about the terrible experiences of the lower realms, as well as all the adverse conditions of the higher realms.

To be born in one of the lower realms of existence as a result of the full maturation of unwholesome actions is called the "fully ripened result."

As experiences are always in accord with their causes, even if one is born in the higher realms, the results of such deeds will be a short life span, poverty, destitution, and so forth. This is called the "experience similar to its cause."

The more one engages in unwholesome deeds, the stronger one's negative conditioning will become, and the habitual patterns thus produced will accompany one from life to life. This will make it increasingly difficult to break free from this vicious circle of conditioning. This is the "action concordant to its cause."

As a result of unwholesome actions the place of one's rebirth will be unpleasant and one will face countless outer obstacles. This is the "result of ownership."

Therefore, "unwholesome deeds" is just another name for inflicting harm upon oneself, a fact I have failed to recognize.

I can remember only a certain number of unwholesome deeds I engaged in during this life, and there are so many more I can't recall. And how often have I incited others to act in unwholesome ways? How often have I rejoiced in the negative deeds of others? But even more than that, I have had countless lives in the past in which I accumulated the imprints of unwholesome deeds upon my mental continuum. Therefore, if I simply let things follow their natural course, I am bound to experience the sufferings of the lower realms.

Until now, unaware of the natural law of cause and result, I have caused harm to myself like a madman. Is this mind of mine wrapped in darkness, or has it come under the influence of some malevolent force? Have I lost my mind? What have I done?

RESOLVE

I now resolve never to commit negative deeds again. If, due to ignorance, I happen to commit any, I shall train myself to immediately disclose and purify them, and not remain associated with such faults for even a single day.

3. Engaging in wholesome deeds

Wholesome actions arise when the mind is free from the three poisons of desire, hatred, and the ignorance concerning the law of cause and result. To refrain from killing, stealing, and sexual misconduct is wholesome physical behavior. The wholesome deeds associated with one's speech are abstaining from lying, divisive talk, hurtful speech, and idle gossip. Not coveting others' possessions and being free of ill will and wrong views are wholesome mental states. When the results of wholesome deeds fully ripen one obtains a rebirth in the higher realms.

The "experience similar to its cause" is then the benefits experienced in those realms, such as longevity, prosperity, and so on.

The "action concordant to its cause," or the conditioning brought about by such deeds, is a natural tendency to perform wholesome deeds, which are the cause of happiness in all future lives.

And the "result of ownership" of virtuous actions is the experience of a physical world endowed with good qualities.

"Wholesome deeds" is just a name for those actions which will bring about my true benefit and happiness. Therefore, the wholesome deeds I have performed, those I caused others to do, and those done by others in which I rejoiced were really worth doing.

RESOLVE

I shall strive with all my heart to act in wholesome ways, paying attention to every single action, insignificant though it may seem. I must proceed without being overpowered by laziness or procrastination. I must do so now, without waiting for a better opportunity.

Deeply contemplate the meaning of these words.

4. Transforming neutral deeds

Many of my actions, such as walking, sleeping, bathing, and the like, are neither negative nor positive by nature. From the point of view of advancing along the path, such actions bear no significant results. By changing the way I relate to those simple deeds, however, I can transform them into wholesome actions that will have a positive impact on my life. I shall therefore make special aspirations relating to my neutral deeds to transform whatever action I can into wholesome deeds.

(For examples of transforming neutral deeds into wholesome activities, see the appendix to this section.)

Brief resolve and supplication for the meditation on karma and its results

This life is short and the time of death unknown. If I let myself come under the influence of negativity or waste my time engaging in insignificant actions, it is like visiting a treasure island and returning with some poisonous food. Consuming it will only harm me. I shall therefore strive as much as possible to abandon unwholesome actions, engage in positive deeds, and transform neutral acts into virtues. I resolve to give my actions a positive direction, without ever coming under the influence of whatever may obstruct my path.

May the Three Precious Jewels guide me so that it will happen in this way.

Introspection

In order to assess our progress we should take a few moments every evening to examine how we have acted during the day. If our body, speech, and mind have been attuned to the Dharma, we should rejoice and reflect on how this was made possible through the kindness of the Three Precious Jewels, and we should commit ourselves to increasing our constructive behavior as much as possible.

If most of our actions are either unwholesome or neutral, we should train in disclosing our negative deeds in front of the objects of refuge (this practice is also called "confession") and contemplate thus:

The reason I can't gain liberation from this world of suffering is that I have been constantly generating mistaken conceptions, resulting in negative conditioning and unwholesome deeds. If I do not change this pattern, there is no certainty that I will be able to gain a rebirth in a higher realm in my next life, let alone liberation and perfect buddhahood.

RESOLVE

From today onwards I commit myself to changing unwholesome and fruitless patterns and courses of action. I will, to the best of my abilities, generate new wholesome behavior and increase the positive actions I already engage in. At the same time I will abandon the unwholesome deeds I have been engaging in in the past, and will prevent new negativities from arising. May the Three Precious Jewels guide me so that it will happen in this way.

Cultivate such thoughts again and again.

To conclude, recite the **dedication prayers:**

By this merit may I attain omniscience.
Defeating the foe, the harmful afflictions,
May I liberate beings from the ocean of samsara,
Disturbed by the waves of birth, old age, sickness, and death.

Just like the heroic Manjushri,
Who knows things just as they are,
And like Samantabhadra too,
May I follow them all in the ways they have trained,
And completely dedicate all these virtues.

Appendix:
Examples of transforming neutral deeds into wholesome activities

When at home one should wish,
"May all living beings attain the city of liberation."

When sitting down,
"May all beings attain the seat of awakening."

When lying down to sleep,
"May all beings attain the dharmakaya of the Buddha."

When rising,
"May all beings attain the nirmanakaya."

When putting on clothes,
"May all beings wear the cloth of self-respect and modesty."

When bathing,
"May all beings wash off the dirt of afflictions."

When eating food,
"May all beings enjoy the nourishment of samadhi."

When leaving the house,
"May all beings be released from the city of samsara."

When going somewhere,
"May all beings take the path of the Noble Ones."

When performing work,
"May all beings complete the two purposes."

When entering one's home,
"May all beings enter the city of liberation."

After arriving at one's destination,
"May all beings reach the stage of buddhahood."

And so on, applying specific wishes adapted to each situation.

5. Longing for true freedom: contemplating the faults of samsara

Having reset our priorities in life and gained conviction in the law of karma and the importance of our motivation, the next step is to contemplate the nature of conditioned existence in general.

In his foundational discourse on the Four Noble Truths the Buddha taught that one of the characteristics of existence is duhkha, which can be translated as "suffering and dissatisfaction" (or simply "suffering"). This truth of suffering is to be clearly understood if one is to engage in a sound spiritual path which aims at transcending it. The contemplation of suffering is not intended to generate a pessimistic outlook on life. On the contrary, it is an objective assessment of experience as we know it, including its inconvenient truths, that will lay the foundation for a path which will enable us to transcend this "reality."

By cultivating an awareness of suffering and the ultimately unsatisfactory nature of conditioned existence we begin to see the major shortcoming of our way of being. This realization will become a driving force for a spiritual path leading to true freedom and the end of suffering.

The contemplation of suffering has three parts, corresponding to the three types of suffering and unsatisfactoriness: obvious suffering, the suffering of change, and the all-pervasive suffering of conditioned existence.

*After the **opening section** contemplate the following:*

1.   Acknowledging suffering in its obvious forms

The reality of suffering, in both its physical and mental forms, is an undeniable part of life. My birth brought with it suffering for myself as well as for my mother.

Then, as I grew up, I experienced all kinds of diseases, some more serious than others—from minor headaches to excruciating pain.

As we get old our bodies grow weak, our senses lose their strength, and as we are more prone to sickness we have to undergo all kinds of treatments related to the ageing of the body.

Finally, the process of death is often accompanied by all sorts of discomfort and pain, not to mention the mental agony caused by the fear of dying.

Mentally we suffer when we encounter unpleasant situations or meet disagreeable or hurtful people, when we lose what is dear to us, and when we are separated from those we love. We suffer when things do not match our expectations, when we do not get or achieve what we want, when we are sad, desperate, stressed, pressured, or depressed.

RESOLVE

I shall not close my eyes to these facts of life. Rather, I shall openly acknowledge the unpleasant aspects of my experience, because the quest for truth and liberation must begin with a realistic view of the world.

Suffering beyond my own

All these forms of suffering are very common for us who are born as humans. However, other forms of life have to undergo much more severe forms of suffering, in terms of both intensity and duration. Animals, for instance, are devoured by each other, abused, enslaved, and slaughtered by humans for their flesh and skin. On top of that, they are generally incapable of differentiating wholesome from unwholesome deeds, which makes it almost impossible for an animal to obtain a rebirth in one of the higher realms of existence.

The form of life called "hungry spirits" results from constant craving and attachment. These beings suffer from the agony of never finding food and drink, and even when they do, the little they find causes them internal pain as they ingest it. They roam the world in constant search for satisfaction, which they never experience, and so they never rest.

Others perceive the world they live in as a hell as a result of the powerful conditioning of hatred and aggression. Such beings suffer unimaginably from physical and mental pain which is said to be much more severe than even the worst sufferings we humans experience.

2.   Reflection on the suffering of change

Of course things are not always unpleasant. There is pleasure in this world: beautiful sights and sounds, delightful smells, delicious tastes, and physical comfort. The question is: How long do these experiences last? Not having given much thought to this, I somehow hope that the happiness I cling to will last forever. In reality, however, all the joy and pleasure I crave is insubstantial and in a state of constant change. Clinging to temporary semblances of happiness as if they were truly satisfactory, I go through all kinds of hardships, exhausting myself in the search for a happiness that never lasts. All of this is based on confusion. Am I not simply deluding myself in this way?

The conditions that bring about our temporary happiness change every moment. Even those considered to be the most fortunate and those who have the greatest wealth have to face the sufferings of birth, old age, sickness, and death, of possibly or actually losing their wealth, of meeting unexpectedly with the unwanted, of parting from what they hold most dear, and of despair.

Knowing this, how can an intelligent person still be attached to the semblance of happiness of this world? Being attached and clinging to it only lead to misery.

Generate the intense resolve to diligently work towards liberation from samsara, like a bird would flee a burning forest.

RESOLVE

Now, whatever it takes, I must practice from the depth of my heart the holy Dharma which certainly liberates from samsara.

3. Reflection on the all-pervasive suffering of conditioned existence

According to the Buddha the only reliable form of happiness is the one that naturally shines forth when the causes of suffering and dissatisfaction are completely uprooted. For this to happen we first need to understand from what it is that we seek freedom. Basically, the Buddha says, all experiences rooted in even the most subtle forms of confusion are fundamentally unsatisfactory, a basis for tension, stress, pain, and all the rest. Suffering may be blatantly obvious and unwanted, or disguised in alluring costumes of pleasure, though not lasting in any way. Underlying each aspect of ordinary, self-centered existence, however, is a network of conditioned experiences, rooted in a fundamental confusion: the misapprehension of who or what I really am. This is what the Buddha called "ignorance." In his *Introduction to the Middle Way* Master Chandrakirti states:

> Firstly with the thought of "I," they cling to self,
> And then with "mine," they grow attached to things,
> Helplessly they wander like a turning waterwheel—
> To compassion for these beings I bow down!

Dissociated from an appreciation of how things really are, unaware of the actuality of my experience, I tend to interpret the world with "me" at the center of the universe, which is a complete hallucination. Everything supporting this deluded sense of "I" is clung to, everything threatening it is rejected. Such thoughts, at odds with the reality of things, produce a constant state of tension. Under this kind of pressure I seek to calm the tensions by any means available, often unskillfully, without inquiring deeply into the nature of these needs. This leads to unwholesome actions, resulting in the experience of dissatisfaction and suffering, for myself and for others.

Don't the problems we run into over and over again seem to follow a certain repetitive kind of pattern? Wouldn't it be wonderful to be totally at ease, free from this constant chase after this or that thing or experience?

RESOLVE

Instead of looking for the next best fix, I resolve to explore the deeper workings of my mind, of my habits and tendencies, in order to find ways to release the heart.

Further reflections:

Over all my lifetimes I have been clinging to body and mind as objects to be cherished, while they are in fact the support for all this suffering. All activities conditioned by this clinging have produced nothing but suffering. In the end there is nothing I could point to as the result of my hard work in search for my own lasting satisfaction and happiness. Having carelessly engaged with all possible objects of desire, not only has my attachment not diminished, but the pain and dissatisfaction brought about by constant desire have increased. Such actions are like adding fuel onto a blazing fire. Have I achieved any form of lasting happiness so far? It is obvious that it cannot be done in this way. I have experienced countless births in all possible realms of existence in search of happiness, but was unable to find true peace and freedom so far. Not only have I not reached the entrance of the path to liberation, but I still have no choice but to continuously roam in samsara, this place of constant change and uncertainty.

There is no one to blame but myself. I have been deceived by myself alone. The suffering I have to endure is the result of my own actions. Unable to entrust my path to the Three Precious Jewels, the nondeceiving protectors, I did not rely on the causes for lasting happiness. Unable to see how much inevitable suffering there is in the world, deceived by uncertain and impermanent forms of happiness, and conditioned by my own delusions, I was distracted by never-ending activities and attached to temporary pleasures. All of this is due to not having generated a deeper understanding of life, a sense of weariness and disenchantment with this circle of confusion and of the suffering of birth and death.

RESOLVE

From now on I must abstain from all worldly activities carried out for the benefit of this life alone. These activities are meaningless, they are devoid of essence. Having directed my mind toward the Precious Jewels, I must enter the path of liberation, relying upon the instructions of virtuous spiritual friends. I shall practice from the depth of my heart the sacred, authentic Dharma, which is the sole means to forever extinguish the fire of suffering.

Thinking thus, pray with intense faith and devotion:

> May the Precious Jewels lead me to practice the holy
> Dharma and progress along the path to liberation.

We should carry out such contemplations sincerely until we are deeply moved and feel absolutely determined to follow the path of liberation in a genuine way. Physical signs may accompany this realization, such as tears coming to our eyes, goose bumps on our skin, and so forth. When such experiences arise, don't let yourself get distracted. Without suppressing them, simply continue the practice. This will produce a genuine longing for liberation from samsara.

*To conclude, recite the **dedication prayers**:*

> By this merit may I attain omniscience.
> Defeating the foe, the harmful afflictions,
> May I liberate beings from the ocean of samsara,
> Disturbed by the waves of birth, old age, sickness,
> and death.

> Just like the heroic Manjushri,
> Who knows things just as they are,

And like Samantabhadra too,
May I follow them all in the ways they have trained,
And completely dedicate all these virtues.

STAGE THREE

A change of heart:
for the benefit of all

6.   Opening the heart: cultivating loving-kindness

The four previous contemplations were aimed at generating the strong wish to attain a state of true freedom from suffering and its causes. The next meditations—on loving-kindness, compassion, and bodhicitta—will help us widen the scope of our motivation, going beyond the concern for our individual liberation.

The first meditation of this second set enables us to generate, deepen, and stabilize one of the most powerful states of mind: loving-kindness, defined as "the wish for beings to be truly happy and to have the causes of happiness." The formal meditation session provides the safe environment necessary to build up the strength of this mental state, allowing it to gradually transform our being. This meditation is practiced in all Buddhist traditions. The instructions presented here follow one of many traditional methods for cultivating a loving heart. This attitude functions as the basis for the cultivation of compassion, which then naturally leads to the generation of bodhicitta, the resolve to attain buddhahood for the sake of all beings.

In the traditional sequence you begin by generating loving-kindness for your mother, followed by other loved and dear ones, those perceived as enemies, and finally for all beings. The idea behind this sequence is to start by thinking of someone very close to one's heart in order to make it easy to generate this positive emotion. This feeling is then extended to other beings.

If, for some reason, you find it difficult to generate loving-kindness for your mother of this life, this approach may not be appropriate. In this case, you should first choose (1) any person who has truly cared for you, someone you naturally feel great gratitude towards. From there you may move on to cultivate loving-kindness for (2) other loved ones, followed by (3) other kind people, (4) enemies or those you don't get on with, and finally (5) all beings.

The important thing to keep in mind is that this practice develops naturally, beginning with an easy object and progressing gradually towards beings we find it increasingly difficult to genuinely care for. In this way, we learn to open the heart step-by-step. If certain events of our past make it difficult or impossible to work in the traditional sequence beginning with one's mother, you may follow the alternative sequence laid out above or seek the guidance of an experienced teacher for further instructions.

The general procedure is always the same: vividly bring the individual to mind, recollect his or her kindness, and think of the need to repay this kindness.

To gradually train in loving-kindness you may devote separate meditation sessions to the individual objects, focusing exclusively on the first object (your mother or your dearest benefactor) during the first few sessions or even weeks of training, then moving on to the second object for the next period, and so forth.

Begin as usual with the **opening section** and then proceed with the cultivation of loving-kindness.

1.   Cultivating loving-kindness for one's mother

This practice has three steps: recalling one's mother, thinking of her kindness, thinking of the need to repay her kindness.

1.1. Thinking of one's mother:

Regardless of whether she is alive or dead, vividly visualize your mother: her general appearance, the details of her face, and the like, just as she is or was. Remember the manner in which she loves and cherishes (or loved and cherished) you, and think with intensity:

This is my kind mother.

1.2. Thinking of her kindness:

This practice has three aspects: thinking of your mother's kindness in giving you your body and life; thinking of her kindness in teaching you how to act in the world, what to do and what not to do; and thinking of her kindness in bearing all kinds of hardships in order to bring you up.

*i. Thinking of her kindness in **giving you your body and life**:*

My mother carried me for nine full months in her womb, enduring all the discomforts and pain of pregnancy. She ate wholesome food and did things that would be beneficial for me, avoiding harmful food and conduct. Then, enduring all the pain of delivery, she gave birth to this body of mine endowed with the prerequisites for the practice of the Dharma. My mother was incredibly kind to me in this way.

To contemplate her kindness in nurturing you, think thus:

As an infant I was absolutely helpless and dependent upon my mother. I was physically powerless to survive on my own; I could not communicate my needs verbally; and I was mentally incapable of differentiating between what is beneficial and what is harmful. I was absolutely helpless. But my mother did not abandon me. She cherished me with all her heart, looked upon me with loving eyes, called me by sweet names, and gently took care of me. She gave me the right kind of food when I was hungry, she gave me something to drink when I was thirsty, she washed my body whenever necessary, warmed me with the warmth of her own body, fed me with sweet milk, protected me from any harm, and guarded me from heat and cold. Missing me whenever we were separated, she nursed me with the deep love and affection unique between mother and child.

ii. *Thinking of her kindness in* **teaching you how to act in the world:**

My mother was my first teacher. She taught me how to eat and drink properly, how to walk and sit, and how to speak and interact with others. Even though I take it for granted now, my mother was so kind in teaching me everything I need to know about how to act in the world, what to do and what not to do. She never gave up on me, no matter how many mistakes I made.

iii. Thinking of her kindness in **bearing all kinds of hardships in order to bring you up:**

Without regard for her own health and welfare, my mother constantly took care that I would not get sick or die. She always wanted me to have only the best of everything. She gave me whatever she could afford, and did her best to make me happy. When I was sick, she cared for me or sought out all possible help, taking me to doctors and specialists to treat my disease. In order to take care of me she gave up her leisure time and even her sleep at night. She worked so hard to assure my well-being, disregarding even her own comfort.

Bringing me up in this way gave her great satisfaction. If she could, she would have offered me all the resources of this world. She always worried about me; my well-being was her main concern. She really took greater care of me than of herself.

It is very rare to even hear the name of the Three Precious Jewels in this world. Beyond that, if one puts the teachings into practice, one will have physical happiness in this life, mental happiness in the intermediate state, a pleasant path in the next life, and will go from happiness to happiness in every lifetime. I owe the opportunity I now have to my mother's kindness.

Also think thus:

My mother has been so kind to me not only in this life, but since beginningless time. As time has no beginning, I have had countless births, and thus she has nourished me with incomparable kindness many, many times. And all these times, instead of working towards her own freedom and ultimate happiness, she devoted herself to bringing me up. How could I ever repay her kindness?

1.3.   Think of the need to repay her kindness:
Then think thus:

What kind of person would I be if I would not try my best to repay my mother's kindness? From now on I shall do everything in my power to repay the kindness she has shown me.

What would be most beneficial for her? In the short term she would be benefited by a healthy body and mind, and in the long run by possessing the causes of happiness, the potential created by wholesome deeds.

Next, generate the thought of loving-kindness in association with either the aspiration, the wish, the resolve, or the supplication. Repeat as many times as possible whichever recitation you find more effective for generating loving-kindness.

i. In association with the **aspiration**, *think thus:*

May she be endowed with true happiness and the causes of happiness! (*Cultivate this thought as many times as possible.*)

*ii. In association with the **wish**, think thus:*

How deeply I wish her to be truly happy and have the causes of happiness! *(Repeat as many times as possible.)*

*iii. In association with the **resolve**, think thus:*

I myself will do all I can to make her obtain true happiness and the causes of happiness. *(Repeat as many times as possible.)*

*iv. In association with the **supplication**, think thus:*

At this point I don't have the power to bring about my mother's happiness or enable her to have the causes of happiness. Only the Three Precious Jewels have this power.

A buddha, an enlightened being, can skillfully show her the path to genuine happiness. The authentic practice of the Dharma can bring about her true happiness, and the Sangha can assist her on this path.

Just as a crippled mother whose only child is being carried away by water yells for help, so one should meditate and pray thus repeatedly:

May the Three Precious Jewels bless my mother. May she be receptive to their transformative influence, which will enable her to gain true happiness and the causes of happiness.

Through practicing in this way you will be able to generate genuine and natural love for your mother. To conclude, recite the **dedication prayers.**

> By this merit may I attain omniscience.
> Defeating the foe, the harmful afflictions,
> May I liberate beings from the ocean of samsara,
> Disturbed by the waves of birth, old age, sickness,
> and death.

> Just like the heroic Manjushri,
> Who knows things just as they are,
> And like Samantabhadra too,
> May I follow them all in the ways they have trained,
> And completely dedicate all these virtues.

2. Loving-kindness for other relatives and loved ones

Apply the same procedure as with your mother. Bring to mind other relatives and loved ones who have been most kind to you, such as your father, siblings, life partner, and so on. Start by visualizing your father, for instance, and recollect his kindness:

(My father, etc.) has been kind to me in so many ways. (He) genuinely cared and provided for me, taught me many things, and protected me from every harm. (He) took care of me in the following ways:

(Here, recollect in detail the ways he or she has cared for you in this life.)

In previous lives too *(he)* has been dear to me, raising and protecting me from harm. *(He)* has been kind to me in so many ways.

After vividly remembering his/her presence and recollecting his/ her kindness, contemplate the need to repay his/her kindness.

I must repay the kindness *(he)* has shown me.

What would be most beneficial for *(him)*? In the short term *(he)* would be benefited by a healthy body and mind, and in the long run by possessing the causes of happiness, the potential created by wholesome deeds.

Repeat the same procedure as above, generating loving-kindness in association with the aspiration, the wish, the resolve, or the supplication, whatever works best.

Cultivate this practice until you generate a love for him or her equal to the love you have for your mother or dearest benefactor.

Then, repeat this exercise with other loved ones. To conclude the session, recite the **dedication prayers.**

> By this merit may I attain omniscience.
> Defeating the foe, the harmful afflictions,
> May I liberate beings from the ocean of samsara,
> Disturbed by the waves of birth, old age, sickness, and death.

Just like the heroic Manjushri,
Who knows things just as they are,
And like Samantabhadra too,
May I follow them all in the ways they have trained,
And completely dedicate all these virtues.

3.　Extending one's loving-kindness to others

Extending the cultivation of loving-kindness to other beings has three parts: meditating on others who have been kind to you (colleagues, neighbors, and so on), meditating on your enemies or people you don't get on with, and finally on all sentient beings.

3.1. Loving-kindness for other kind people:

Bring to mind other beings, like colleagues, neighbors, and others who have been kind in some way or another. Think of each being individually; recollect the kindness of each; and think how you can repay him or her:

(*She*) has benefited me in the following ways:

(*Here, recollect the ways each has benefited you.*)

And in previous lives (*she*) has been my parent many times, taking me under (*her*) care. (*She*) has been kind to me in so many different ways. What would be most beneficial for (*her*)?

In the short term (*she*) would be benefited by a healthy body and mind, and in the long run by possessing the causes of happiness, the potential created by wholesome deeds.

Again, generate loving-kindness in association with the aspiration, the wish, the resolve, or the supplication. Repeat the exercise with other individuals.

*To conclude the session, recite the **dedication prayers**.*

> By this merit may I attain omniscience.
> Defeating the foe, the harmful afflictions,
> May I liberate beings from the ocean of samsara,
> Disturbed by the waves of birth, old age, sickness,
> and death.
>
> Just like the heroic Manjushri,
> Who knows things just as they are,
> And like Samantabhadra too,
> May I follow them all in the ways they have trained,
> And completely dedicate all these virtues.

3.2. Loving-kindness for one's enemies:

The way to extend the meditation on loving-kindness to your enemies is to bring to mind those who have caused you harm, who are the objects of aversion and hatred, and think thus:

The beings I perceive as my enemies have been my kind parents many times in previous lives, and each time they benefited me in many ways, protecting me from every harm. But having failed to repay their kindness, I perceive these beings who pressure me to repay the debts of previous lives as enemies, just as a debtor perceives his creditors to be abusive when pressured to repay his debts.

Since our minds are obscured by karma, mental afflictions, and the change from one life to another, we don't recognize each other but see each other as harmer and harmed. Our minds are deluded in this way. Though we are actually very close, we end up harming each other because we are under the power of afflictions. For this reason the gap created between us has become wider and wider.

And even now, my so-called "enemies" help me crush my pride, cultivate tolerance, and purify my negative karma of the past. Indeed, even now they support me in various ways. Instead of harming them back I will pray for their happiness and peace.

What would be most beneficial for them?

In the short term they would be benefited by a healthy body and mind, and in the long run by possessing the causes of happiness, the potential created by wholesome deeds.

*Again, generate loving-kindness in association with the aspiration, the wish, the resolve, or the supplication. To conclude the session, recite the **dedication prayers**.*

By this merit may I attain omniscience.
Defeating the foe, the harmful afflictions,
May I liberate beings from the ocean of samsara,
Disturbed by the waves of birth, old age, sickness, and death.

Just like the heroic Manjushri,
Who knows things just as they are,

And like Samantabhadra too,
May I follow them all in the ways they have trained,
And completely dedicate all these virtues.

3.3. Loving-kindness for all sentient beings:

To extend loving-kindness to all sentient beings, think thus:

Space is boundless and the beings inhabiting the myriad worlds in it are also countless. Time is without beginning, so I have had countless lives in the past.

There is therefore not a single sentient being who hasn't once been my mother. They have all been my parents on many occasions, and each time they have truly cared for me, protecting me from harm. Still, I cannot recognize that they were my parents because my mind is obscured by karma, the afflictions, and the change from one life to another. The indifference I feel towards most beings is not right. I should repay their kindness by kindness and their benefit by benefit, as much as I can.

What would be most beneficial for them?

In the short term they would be benefited by a healthy body and mind, and in the long run by possessing the causes of happiness, the potential created by wholesome deeds.

Again, generate loving-kindness in association with the aspiration, the wish, the resolve, or the supplication.

*To conclude, recite the **dedication prayers**:*

By this merit may I attain omniscience.
Defeating the foe, the harmful afflictions,
May I liberate beings from the ocean of samsara,
Disturbed by the waves of birth, old age, sickness,
and death.

Just like the heroic Manjushri,
Who knows things just as they are,
And like Samantabhadra too,
May I follow them all in the ways they have trained,
And completely dedicate all these virtues.

Having meditated in this way, if you produce a genuine desire to benefit all the sentient beings throughout endless space, then your meditation on loving-kindness has been accomplished.

In between meditation sessions you should abandon anger toward any sentient beings and look upon them affectionately, as a loving mother looks upon her cherished child. To those who live in fear, you should give protection and comfort, and save the lives of those about to be killed and so on. To those who are destitute, give food, shelter, and so on, and converse with them in a gentle and pleasing voice. For animals, you should recite into their ears the names of buddhas and mantras.

7. Cultivating compassion

Compassion is the wish for beings to be free of suffering and its causes. The practice described here follows the traditional sequence, beginning, as in the practice of loving-kindness, with cultivating compassion for one's mother. If this proves difficult or inefficient, you may first focus on another benefactor who has cared for you and for whom it feels natural to have compassion.

Again, train gradually by devoting separate sessions to the individual objects of compassion.

*Begin as usual with the **opening section**.*

1.   Cultivating compassion for one's mother

You begin this practice, as in the cultivation of loving-kindness, by visualizing your mother in front of you and recollecting her kindness. For a clear outline, please review steps 1.1. (i.e., thinking of one's mother) and 1.2. (recalling her kindness) in the previous meditation.

Then think thus:

My kind mother has cared for me and benefited me in so many ways in this life, and in countless past lives as well. She benefited and protected me from harm each time. Instead of looking after herself in the search for a path to true happiness, she constantly worked for my welfare and has therefore not been able to escape from samsara.

Right now she is experiencing suffering, even though she just wants to be happy. She does not know how to free herself from suffering and actively engages in the various causes of future sorrow. How sad this is!

My mother developed great attachment for me, her child, and hatred towards those who opposed or belittled me. She may even have engaged in unwholesome deeds like killing or stealing for my sake due to these emotions. As a result of these actions she is still caught in ignorance, dissatisfaction, and suffering, and in future lives she faces possible rebirths in miserable states of existence. This is truly pitiful!

I need to repay her kindness with kindness and her benefit with benefit. What would be most beneficial for her? She would be benefited directly by being free from suffering, and indirectly by having the causes of her suffering removed.

However, she is clearly experiencing suffering in this life as a result of her past negative actions, and she actively engages in unwholesome deeds with body, speech, and mind, planting the seeds for the experience of future suffering and dissatisfaction. This is so sad!

Now generate compassion in association with either the aspiration, the wish, the resolve, or the supplication, whichever works best for you. Repeat each thought as many times as possible.

*i. In association with the **aspiration**, think thus:*

May she be free from suffering and from its causes, which are unwholesome deeds and afflictions.

May she be free from the concepts of "I" and "mine," which are the root of contaminated karma and afflictions.

May she also be free from the ignorance which clings to things as inherently existent.

*ii. In association with the **wish**, think thus:*

How deeply I wish that she be free from suffering and from the causes of suffering, which are unwholesome deeds and afflictions.

How deeply I wish that she be free from the concepts of "I" and "mine," the root of contaminated karma and afflictions.

How deeply I wish that she be free from the ignorance which clings to things as inherently existent.

*iii. In association with the **resolve**, think thus:*

I will help her gain the state that is free from suffering and its causes, which are unwholesome deeds and afflictions.

I will free her from the concepts of "I" and "mine," the root of contaminated karma and afflictions.

I will also free her from the ignorance which clings to things as inherently existent.

*iv. In association with the **supplication**, think thus:*

Even though she is worn out by the sufferings of this world, she keeps accumulating unwholesome karma and nurturing her mental afflictions, which are the causes of future suffering. How sad and truly pitiful!

Although I want to place her in a state free from suffering and its causes, I lack the ability to accomplish this. Only the Three Precious Jewels have this power.

May the Three Precious Jewels bless her so that she becomes free from suffering and the causes of suffering, unwholesome deeds and afflictions.

May the Three Precious Jewels bless her so that she becomes free from the concepts of "I" and "mine," the root of contaminated karma and afflictions.

May the Three Precious Jewels bless her so that she may also be free from the ignorance which clings to things as inherently existent.

*To conclude the session, recite the **dedication prayers**.*

2.   Cultivating compassion for others

2.1. *Likewise, cultivate compassion for your **other relatives**, **and for those who are manifestly experiencing** **suffering or are engaged in unwholesome deeds**, which are the causes of future suffering. Generate compassion and cultivate this practice as explained above.*

2.2. *To cultivate compassion for your **enemies** or people you don't get on with, think thus:*

(*She/he*) has also been my mother many times, and each time (*she/he*) has been very kind to me, benefiting and protecting me in many ways.

Follow the same procedure as explained above. Then think thus:

Though *(she/he)* is harming me now, I feel compassion for *(her/him)* because *(her/his)* mind is now deluded and *(she/he)* has failed to recognize me as *(her/his)* child.

Not only that but, having no control over *(her/his)* own mind, *(her/his)* harming me becomes the cause for *(her/him)* to experience the sufferings of miserable states of existence in the future. How sad!

As above, generate compassion in association with the aspiration, the wish, the resolve, or the supplication.

2.3. *Likewise, think of the* **beings of the six realms** *(i.e., beings in the divine realms, demigods, humans, animals, hungry spirits, and hell beings) and their corresponding sufferings.*

Following the same procedure, consider how each of them acted as your mother in previous lives, bringing you up with great care. Reflect on their current difficulties and all the suffering they have to undergo, and generate the desire to repay their kindness.

To conclude, recite the **dedication prayers***:*

By this merit may I attain omniscience.
Defeating the foe, the harmful afflictions,
May I liberate beings from the ocean of samsara,
Disturbed by the waves of birth, old age, sickness,
and death.

Just like the heroic Manjushri,
Who knows things just as they are,

And like Samantabhadra too,
May I follow them all in the ways they have trained,
And completely dedicate all these virtues.

When the wish to free all beings from suffering has become powerful and stable, one has given birth to great compassion, the principal cause for the arising of bodhicitta.

8. Bodhicitta: generating the resolve to become a buddha

*Bodhicitta, the resolve to become a buddha in order to be able to perfectly guide beings along the path to happiness and awakening, is the natural outcome of the cultivation of great loving-kindness and great compassion. To familiarize yourself with and strengthen this resolve, begin by **going for refuge**.*

Then, contemplate the following:

All beings without exception desire happiness and do not want to suffer. In this regard we are all the same and share the same plight in our search for lasting happiness and peace. But although all these beings who have all been my kind parents in the past do not want to suffer, they do not know the right methods to fulfill this fundamental wish. Countless beings are experiencing suffering right now and countless also are engaging in unwholesome deeds, creating the causes of future suffering.

They are blinded by ignorance, unable to rely on the path that would free them from suffering and its causes. Lacking a skillful teacher's guidance, they turn their backs on the path of liberation and the happiness of the higher realms. Instead, they constantly produce suffering for themselves and others, sowing the seeds for the experience of miserable states of existence. This is truly pitiful!

Dwell upon such thoughts until a genuine feeling of compassion for all beings arises in you. Then think thus:

However, just saying "how pitiful" will not be of benefit.

I must free them from suffering and its causes, and establish them in the state of true happiness.

At present, I clearly lack the power and the means to do so. Only a buddha, perfect in wisdom, compassion, and skillful means, truly has this ability.

A single Dharma discourse given by a buddha can liberate countless beings from ignorance, the root of all suffering, and even just the sight of an Awakened One has inconceivable benefits.

By teaching the law of karma, actions and their results, a buddha sets beings on the path to temporary happiness, and by teaching them the methods to realize ultimate reality, he enables them to attain liberation from samsara. What greater benefit can there be?

Directly or indirectly coming into contact with a buddha—by seeing, hearing, remembering, or touching an Awakened One, countless beings gain the ability to accomplish their most fundamental wishes: happiness and freedom from suffering.

How wonderful would it be if I could attain the stage of buddhahood, perfect awakening, for the sake of all sentient beings! *(Cultivate this aspiration as many times as possible.)*

Whatever it takes, I now resolve to attain this sublime state of perfect awakening for the sake of all beings. *(Repeat this commitment as many times as possible.)*

Dwell deeply on such thoughts again and again to generate the firm resolve to become a buddha in order to free beings from the sufferings of samsara.

Then, sincerely think thus:

Having gained buddhahood, I will skillfully guide beings along the path of liberation according to their capacities and dispositions. In the short term I will lead them to temporary happiness according to their dispositions, and ultimately to the state of perfect buddhahood as well.

Then pray very intensely:

> May the Three Jewels guide me so that I can make this happen!

*To conclude, recite the **dedication prayers**:*

> By this merit may I attain omniscience.
> Defeating the foe, the harmful afflictions,
> May I liberate beings from the ocean of samsara,
> Disturbed by the waves of birth, old age, sickness,
> and death.
>
> Just like the heroic Manjushri,
> Who knows things just as they are,
> And like Samantabhadra too,
> May I follow them all in the ways they have trained,
> And completely dedicate all these virtues.

Also, in between the meditation sessions, constantly recall the wonderful qualities of buddhahood, and generate the intense wish to fully awaken for the benefit of all beings.

Appendix:
Taking the bodhicitta vow

According to Shantideva's The Way of the Bodhisattva:

To deepen and stabilize this practice it is very helpful to formally take the bodhicitta vow. It is advisable to first receive it from a lineage master of the living tradition, but it may also be taken by following the steps laid out below. After one has taken it one should be mindful to guard this vow by observing the commitments related to it. For further details please consult the relevant literature.[1]

This little ritual can also become a daily practice, repeated during each of the six or four sessions in a day, or at least in the morning and in the evening. Begin by reciting the Seven-Limb Prayer, followed by the practice of going for refuge. After this, generate the bodhicitta of aspiration and applied bodhicitta as taught in Shantideva's The Way of the Bodhisattva.

The Seven-Limb Prayer *(recite three times):*

> To you, supreme objects of refuge, I pay homage,
> And I worship you, offering vast clouds of emanated offerings,
> Just like Samantabhadra did.
> In front of you I openly lay bare all negativities
> I accumulated in this cycle of existence without beginning,
> And in all wholesome and meritorious deeds of others I wholeheartedly rejoice.

---

1   Refer for instance to Shantideva (2006), Kunzang Pelden (2010), and Jamgön Kongtrül (2003).

You buddhas and your heirs I entreat to teach us the
Dharma,
And I supplicate you: Please remain, do not pass
beyond into nirvana!
All virtue thus accumulated I dedicate to all beings
So they may gain the state of perfect awakening.

Taking the bodhicitta vow

*While reciting the next three stanzas, focus your mind on the
objects of refuge from whom you take the bodhicitta vow.*

To all the buddhas, all the Blessed Ones of ten
directions, to all the bodhisattva-mahasattvas of the
ten grounds, and to the gurus, great Vajradharas, I
pray: Please think of me!

Until the essence of enlightenment is reached
I go for refuge to the buddhas.
Also I take refuge in the Dharma
And in all the host of bodhisattvas.

Just as all the buddhas of the past have given birth to
bodhicitta,
And step-by-step abode and trained in the
bodhisattvas' precepts,
Likewise, for the benefit of beings, I too will give
birth to bodhicitta,
And I will abide and train myself in those precepts
step-by-step.

(Repeat the preceding three times.)

Today my life has given fruit.
This human state has now been well assumed.
Today I take my birth in Buddha's line,
And have become the Buddha's child and heir.

In every way, then,
I will undertake activities befitting such a rank.
And I will do no act to mar or compromise
This high and faultless lineage.

And so, today, within the sight of all protectors,
I summon beings, calling them to buddhahood.
And, till that state is reached, to every earthly joy!
May gods and demigods and all the rest rejoice!

May bodhicitta, precious and sublime,
Arise where it has not yet come to be.
And where it has arisen may it never fail,
But grow and flourish even more.

To conclude, recite the **dedication prayers:**

By this merit may I attain omniscience.
Defeating the foe, the harmful afflictions,
May I liberate beings from the ocean of samsara,
Disturbed by the waves of birth, old age, sickness,
and death.

Just like the heroic Manjushri,
Who knows things just as they are,
And like Samantabhadra too,
May I follow them all in the ways they have trained,
And completely dedicate all these virtues.

9.   Applied bodhicitta in meditation, part 1: cultivating equality between oneself and others

The practices of applied bodhicitta are designed to remedy the errors on the Mahayana path, i.e., self-cherishing (subdued by means of equalizing and exchanging self and others) and self-grasping (uprooted by means of the union of calm abiding and superior insight).

Cultivating equality between oneself and others counteracts the tendency to think that we are more important than others, that we are in the center of the universe so to speak. Since this equality functions as the basis for the practice of exchanging, it is recommended to familiarize oneself with this state of mind before moving on to the next step.

Start by going for refuge as before, followed by the generation of bodhicitta (recite three times):

> For the sake of all sentient beings throughout endless space I must achieve the precious state of perfect buddhahood. For this purpose I will practice this profound path.

Then contemplate in the following way:

Even though I deeply wish to gain the state of unsurpassable enlightenment for the sake of all sentient beings, unless I am able to destroy self-grasping and transform all my activities of body, speech, and mind to benefit sentient beings, this goal will stay out of my reach.

Therefore, from now on I shall abandon the attitude of self-cherishing, which is the root of all negativities. (*Recite this resolve three times.*)

The practices of equality and exchanging oneself for others are the most excellent means for transforming all my activities into benefit for all beings. I shall rely on this method, which is the sole path traversed by all bodhisattvas, the Buddha's heirs.

For the practice of equalizing oneself and others, dwell on the following thoughts until the sincere wish to accomplish beings' happiness and to dispel their suffering arises in you. Recite the following as many times as possible:

Just as I desire happiness, so do all sentient beings without exception want to be truly happy. Therefore, starting from today, I will assist all beings to achieve happiness along with its causes.

Just as I do not want to suffer, so do all sentient beings without exception wish to be free of suffering. Therefore, starting from today, I will assist all beings to dispel suffering along with its causes.

With sincere longing think thus:

I sincerely want this to happen, with all my heart.

*To conclude, recite the **dedication prayers:***

By this merit may I attain omniscience.
Defeating the foe, the harmful afflictions,
May I liberate beings from the ocean of samsara,
Disturbed by the waves of birth, old age, sickness,
and death.

Just like the heroic Manjushri,
Who knows things just as they are,
And like Samantabhadra too,
May I follow them all in the ways they have trained,
And completely dedicate all these virtues.

10. Applied bodhicitta in meditation, part 2: exchanging oneself for others

The practice of exchanging oneself for others is also called "the swift path to awakening." Considered the supreme means to subdue the attitude of self-cherishing, which is the direct outcome of clinging to the concepts of "I" and "mine," this practice is cultivated by all bodhisattvas.

*Again, start by **going for refuge** and generating the right **motivation** for the practice (recite three times):*

> For the sake of all sentient beings throughout endless space I must achieve the precious state of perfect buddhahood. For this purpose I will practice this profound path.

1.   The practice of *tonglen* with one's mother

Begin, as with the earlier practice of loving-kindness, by clearly visualizing your mother (or, in case this is not suitable, your dearest benefactor), recollecting her kindness and thinking of the need to repay her kindness:

> My mother gave me this precious body and life through which enlightenment can be achieved. She protected me from harm and fear. She cared deeply for me and benefited me in so many ways, always concerned about my happiness. She has acted in this way not only in this life, but on every occasion she has been my mother in the past since beginningless time. In this way she has shown me immeasurable care and worked for my benefit again and again. Yet she herself is still roaming in this world of suffering devoid of lasting satisfaction. How sad this is!

From this time on I will strive to attain the stage of perfect awakening, the omniscient state of buddhahood, for the sake of my mother.

The reason I have failed to gain buddhahood until now is that I have neglected my kind mother and have mainly nurtured an attitude of self-cherishing. Now, in this short life, I will subdue this negative and unwholesome conditioning. I will cease obeying its commands and being its servant.

I will try my best to repay my mother's kindness by practicing the Dharma, subduing my self-cherishing by exchanging self for others.

All the suffering and the causes of suffering which harm my mother now and in the future I will take upon myself and offer her in return the potential of all my wholesome deeds and my well-being.

Then, recite as many times as possible:

> May all of my kind mother's sufferings and her unwholesome deeds, afflictions, and ignorance, the causes of suffering, ripen upon me!

Imagine that both her suffering and its causes take the form of black smoke which you inhale through your nose. Think that it is absorbed into the center of your heart, where it vanishes without leaving a trace. In this way free your mother from all suffering along with its causes.

Then think thus:

What would truly benefit my mother? She would be

benefited by the experience of happiness and by possessing the causes of happiness.

Therefore, I will give her all my happiness and the potential of my wholesome deeds, the causes of happiness.

Recite as many times as possible:

> May all my happiness and the potential of my wholesome deeds ripen upon my mother!

Imagine that all of your happiness and the potential of your wholesome deeds issue from your heart like the rays of the rising sun and exit through your nostrils. As the light rays touch your mother she instantly enjoys great happiness and well-being. Having further assembled all the favorable conditions to practice the Dharma and increase her virtue, she gains the potential to achieve buddhahood.

If your visualization becomes clearer as a result of this heartfelt practice of sending and taking, you can recite the following short prayer accompanied by the appropriate visualizations:

> May my mother's suffering along with its causes ripen upon me; and by my virtue may she obtain happiness and well-being!

Finally, sincerely think thus:

May she be truly happy and endowed with the causes of happiness; may she be free of suffering and the causes of suffering; and may she swiftly gain buddhahood.

2. The practice of *tonglen* with other beings

Then apply this procedure to different beings, as in the previous practices, beginning with your father, then other dear relatives, friends, enemies, and finally all beings:

(My father, etc.) is suffering against (his) wishes and does not have the means to permanently free (himself) from this miserable condition. This is so sad!

Furthermore, think thus:

From now on I will strive to gain the stage of the perfect awakening of buddhahood for (his) sake.

Follow the same procedure as explained above, and meditate on the visualization of sending and taking as before.

3. Conclusion

Finally, to seal your practice with the right view, think thus:

Although the three elements in this practice—i.e., the individual who is the object of this meditation, oneself who is the agent, and the happiness and suffering that are being exchanged—do not exist in the ultimate sense, they do appear on the conventional level due to the mind's delusion. In the grip of this delusion, beings suffer tremendously. How truly sad this is!

Then pray:

For the sake of all beings trapped in confusion may
I quickly attain the stage of buddhahood, perfect
awakening.

*Close the session by **dedicating** the positive potential generated
by this practice to the attainment of buddhahood for the sake of
all beings and recite the dedication prayers:*

By this merit may I attain omniscience.
Defeating the foe, the harmful afflictions,
May I liberate beings from the ocean of samsara,
Disturbed by the waves of birth, old age, sickness,
and death.

Just like the heroic Manjushri,
Who knows things just as they are,
And like Samantabhadra too,
May I follow them all in the ways they have trained,
And completely dedicate all these virtues.

Appendix:
Khenchen Appey Rinpoche on *tonglen*

In his commentary on *Mind Training in Seven Points* Khenchen Appey Rinpoche explains the practice of exchange and of **sending and taking** in the following way:

In the practice of exchange, **sending** means that one gives away everything, one's body along with one's possessions and the virtues accumulated in the three times, with the wish that this will bring about the conducive conditions for all sentient beings to obtain buddhahood. By **taking**, one takes upon oneself all the suffering and the causes of suffering of all sentient beings, wishing that in this way all beings may be free of suffering and its causes. Thus, one trains by alternating both, which means that one practices sending and taking in turn.

Occasionally we should cultivate sending and taking by mounting them on the wind horse, which is the breath. While breathing in through the nose, think that you are absorbing into your heart the negative deeds and suffering of all beings in the form of black smoke. While breathing out through the nose, think that all your happiness and virtues take the form of white light which reaches all beings, and that this brings about all the conditions necessary for them to attain enlightenment.

STAGE FOUR

Learning to see

11. Bringing the mind home: the practice of shamatha, calm abiding

The meditations on (1) the difficulty of obtaining a precious human life, (2) death and impermanence, (3) the natural law of karma—cause and result, and (4) the faults of samsara form the first set of contemplations, designed to bring about a fundamental change in our outlook on life and the wish to become free from conditioned existence as a whole.

The second set of meditations—on loving-kindness, compassion, and conventional bodhicitta—widen the scope of our practice, opening our hearts to the fundamental needs of all beings.

These two sets lay the necessary foundations for the advanced practices of ultimate bodhicitta, i.e., shamatha ("calm abiding") and vipashyana ("superior insight"), creating the necessary inner conditions for these practices to become fruitful.

Once we have resolved to free ourselves from samsara, and not only for our own sake but in order to benefit all beings in the best possible way by becoming a buddha ourselves, we need the right method for achieving this, which is none other than the union of shamatha and vipashyana. The function of shamatha meditation is to develop a state of deep concentration, clear and stable, free of both mental torpor and unrest. Only a mind equipped with the power of one-pointed concentration combined with superior insight is able to cut through the root of all delusion, clearly seeing the nature of ultimate reality.

In order for shamatha training to be fruitful it is important to live in a suitable, quiet environment, to have time to devote oneself to the practice, to have few needs, and to maintain a pure discipline *as a support. Then, letting go of all thoughts about the past and projections into the future, the training in mental stillness can begin.*

1.   The object of concentration

Theoretically, any stable, unmoving object may be used as a support to develop mental clarity and stability. In this tradition, however, the following three are recommended: a beautiful image of Buddha Shakyamuni (to strengthen one's connection with the object of refuge); the image of a blue flower with four petals (blue is considered soothing to the eye); or simply a blue piece of cloth. The object should be placed at a convenient distance in front of you, about an arm's length away.

2.   The body: the sevenfold posture

Our posture during the practice functions as a support for the mind to relax and at the same time remain alert and vigilant.

Ideally we should adopt the sevenfold posture:

Fully crossed (or half-crossed) legs, to form a stable foundation (if this is not possible it is acceptable to sit on a chair with both feet parallel on the ground);

Hands in the gesture of equanimity resting on your lap about four finger-breadths below the navel, the right hand on top of the left, both palms facing up, and tips of the thumbs slightly touching;

Spine very straight, to prevent sluggishness;

Shoulders held back slightly, gently opening the chest;

Chin tucked in, to gently stretch the neck muscles;

Tip of the tongue touching the palate behind the front teeth, to prevent the production of excessive saliva as well as the sensation of thirst;

Eyes kept slightly open and without blinking, the gaze directed down towards the object of meditation, or about four finger-breadths in front of the nose. This is to prevent sleepiness as well as mental unrest.

You should also keep your **breathing** natural, not manipulating the flow of inhalation and exhalation in any way.

It is important to find the right balance in one's posture which will allow one to relax and remain alert at the same time. Too tense a posture held for too long will produce excessive thoughts, mental unrest, and eventually physical pain. Keeping the body too lax, on the other hand, will induce mental torpor and lack of clarity.

3.   The mind: nine ways to settle the mind

The objective of shamatha practice is to bring the mind to rest in its natural radiance, free of all discursive thinking. To this end there are nine ways to place the mind on the chosen object of meditation:

1. Placing the mind: this is the initial focusing of the mind, achieved by looking at the object of concentration with a relaxed and unblinking gaze. It is important not to think about the features of the object, but to merely use it as a support and to place the mind on it.

2. Continuous placement: as it is difficult for beginners to sustain concentration over extended periods of time, you should focus on the object only for short periods of time, gradually building up the power of concentration. The duration of this may vary between ten seconds and one minute, taking microbreaks between each placement.

3. Repairing and placing again: at this stage one starts working with obstacles arising during concentration by quickly recognizing distraction and redirecting the mind back to the object of meditation. The mind still disengages from the object of concentration when distracted, if only briefly.

4. Close placement: now, even though you are still prone to distraction, the power of mindfulness prevents you from completely losing sight of the object, even when distracted. Your attention span increases and as soon as distraction is recognized, the mind is redirected to the object with refreshed focus.

5. Subduing: when torpor or unrest prevents the mind from entering deeper states of concentration, one applies the appropriate antidotes to subdue these obstacles. The delight you start to experience at this point inspires you to exert yourself in the practice.

6. Pacifying: at this stage there is no more resistance against the training and you keep refining your concentration, pacifying distractions as soon as they arise by directing the mind to the object of meditation. The intensity of involuntary streams of thoughts is very weak at this point and they only occasionally interrupt your concentration (they are not strong enough to completely disengage the mind from the object after the fourth stage).

7. Thorough pacification: even though coarse obstacles do not arise any longer, the mind may still be brought off-balance by subtle dullness and agitation. When this occurs you still need to make an effort to adjust the quality of attention to the object of meditation.

8. Making the mind one-pointed: once the obstacles to concentration (coarse, middling, and subtle) have been eliminated, the mind has gained the ability to remain one-pointedly with the object for the entire duration of the meditation session (about three hours or longer at this point). After the initial placement of the mind, which still requires a subtle effort, this state is sustained effortlessly.

9. Perfectly balanced attention: at this stage, one effortlessly enters the state of meditative absorption, perfectly still and clear, as a result of the training. When this state is sustained until the bliss of mental and physical pliancy arises, one attains the genuine state of shamatha—calm abiding. This state of temporary freedom from afflictions should then be utilized for the training in superior insight.

4. Overcoming obstacles

There are five obstacles to developing shamatha, remedied by means of eight antidotes (given in *italics* below).

The first obstacle, laziness, prevents one from starting the practice in the first place, and the second, not remembering the instructions, prevents one from actually entering the stages of concentration. The next three obstacles occur during the practice of concentration: torpor and unrest, nonapplication of the appropriate antidotes, and overapplication of the antidotes.

1. Laziness is a lack of interest in and enthusiasm for the practice. This obstacle is remedied through developing *interest* in the practice, which is rooted in the *conviction* that this is a worthwhile endeavor (understanding the benefits of concentration and the faults of distraction); and by *diligent effort* in the practice, which will result in a state of *physical and mental pliancy* (free of physical fatigue and mental hindrances, body and mind are rendered perfectly serviceable for the cultivation of shamatha and other wholesome states).

2. Not remembering the instructions is remedied by *recollecting or being mindful* of the meditation object and the instructions on how to focus on it.

3. Torpor and unrest are remedied by the *alertness* which simply recognizes that the mind is in a state of distraction, be it of a coarse or subtle nature.

4. Nonapplication of the antidotes (when the mind has come under the influence of torpor or unrest) is remedied by *applying the appropriate antidotes*.

5. Overapplication of the antidotes (which means that one is still applying antidotes even though the obstacles of torpor or unrest have already been pacified) is remedied by letting go of the antidote and *placing the mind in a balanced way* on the object of meditation.

Remedying mental torpor and unrest

To remedy **torpor** one is advised to reduce the quantity of food eaten before the meditation sessions, to use an elevated seat and a thin cushion, to wear thinner clothes to prevent excessive body heat, and to recite refuge and supplication prayers in a loud voice. When you notice mental torpor arising during the meditation session, tense the body, sit a bit more straight, and make your attention a bit wider, not focusing too tightly on the object.

In case of **unrest**, the opposite methods will eliminate the problem.

When you are unable to remedy the obstacle, take a break, refresh yourself or relax a bit, think again of the benefits of this training and of the faults of a distracted mind, and resume the practice later.

When torpor and unrest have been pacified, meditate in a relaxed state.

5. Five experiences of meditation

1. Waterfall: the recognition that one has a continuous stream of thoughts. This experience may be surprising and overwhelming at first, but it really constitutes the first authentic meditative experience. It is not that you have more thoughts than before, but you notice for the first time how many involuntary thoughts actually occupy the mind.

2. Water in a deep gorge: the stream of thoughts comes to rest from time to time. Continuing your meditation, you will notice how one thought follows the next. At some points this chain of thoughts will break and the mind will be at rest for a short while, before the next stream of thoughts takes over, and so on, alternating between thoughts and stillness.

3. Pool of converging rivers: at this point one mainly experiences a clear state of consciousness devoid of discursive thinking. But this state is still occasionally interrupted by a sudden stream of thoughts.

4. Lake with waves: the stillness of the mind is now interrupted by the arising of only one or two consecutive thoughts. These thoughts are immediately recognized and brought to rest.

5. Perfectly still lake: by sustaining this state eventually all thoughts completely disappear and the sparkling clarity of consciousness arises in this state of one-pointed concentration. At this point one should bring the mind to rest in its natural radiance alone and remain in this state.

6.   The meditation session

In an isolated place, seated upon a comfortable cushion in the sevenfold meditation posture, recite the **refuge and supplication prayers**, *followed by the generation of* **bodhicitta:**

> For the sake of all sentient beings throughout endless space I must achieve the precious state of perfect buddhahood. For this purpose I will practice this profound path. (*Recite three times.*)

Then think thus:

From beginningless time until now my mind has been blown around by the wind of conceptualization. I had no control whatsoever over this mind. Under the influence of delusion it hardly ever had any interest in wholesome things, running after instant gratification of the senses. This is why I am still caught in this ocean of samsara, completely helpless and absolutely unable to help others on the path to liberation.

Now, having received instructions from a spiritual friend, I must exert myself in the purification of body and mind in order to obtain the bliss of liberation and the most exalted state of buddhahood for the sake of all beings. I will train my mind to rest one-pointedly in its natural radiance. This will allow me to eventually obtain the great enlightenment.

If necessary, start with pacifying excessive discursive thinking by counting twenty-one cycles of inhalation and exhalation, and then begin with the training.

Remember the instructions for shamatha meditation and place the mind on the object of meditation without coming under the power of torpor or unrest. If you apply too much effort, the mind will become agitated, in which case you should relax it a bit, without losing your recollection and alertness. If the mind is too relaxed, it will lead to torpor. Applying the antidotes for torpor and unrest whenever necessary, learn to place the mind in the state of perfectly balanced attention once all forms of coarse and subtle distractions are pacified.

When all conceptual thinking has subsided and the mind is still, shift the focus inwardly on the clarity of the mind, the luminous cognitive aspect of consciousness which perceives the object, without closing your eyes or removing the object. When this experience becomes very vivid and you are completely undistracted from the mind's luminosity, relax the mind in this experience.

Do not linger on the past, do not think about the future, and do not keep track of your present activities. Completely cut through all conceptualization, and remain at ease and attentive. Do not overdo it. Continue the meditation session as long as the quality of the practice is still good, taking care to end it before negative feelings arise.

At the end of each session **dedicate** its positive potential to the attainment of buddhahood for the sake of all beings:

> By this merit may I attain omniscience.
> Defeating the foe, the harmful afflictions,
> May I liberate beings from the ocean of samsara,
> Disturbed by the waves of birth, old age, sickness,
> and death.

> Just like the heroic Manjushri,
> Who knows things just as they are,
> And like Samantabhadra too,
> May I follow them all in the ways they have trained,
> And completely dedicate all these virtues.

Then take a break and refresh yourself.

Even in between meditation sessions do not break the continuity of isolation. Discard all the causes of distraction and outwardly directed activities of the mind, and quickly enter the next meditation session. In the beginning, make meditation sessions short, but repeat them many times. When you become habituated, *prolong the sessions until you can keep one continuous meditation session going for three to four hours. In this way you will be able to perfect the training in shamatha.*

12. Seeing reality as it is: the practice of vipashyana, superior insight

The cultivation of superior insight, or vipashyana, is the most profound of all Buddhist practices. Being the direct antidote to ignorance, it has the power to eradicate the latencies of mental afflictions and the root cause of all suffering. For this tool to be effective, however, the mind needs to be well trained in all the preceding meditations, in particular the training in shamatha, and one should also have a sound theoretical understanding of the philosophical view of ultimate reality associated with this practice.

With the cultivation of insight we learn to familiarize ourselves with a profound understanding of the nature of experience. The first step in this process is to question the nature of the self, this fundamental point of reference in our experience, and to see in what way it exists. One then proceeds to question how the experience of the duality of apprehended phenomena and the apprehending subject (the "self") is brought about. This leads to an analysis of the function of the mind in this process and of its true nature.

Even though the meditation presented here does offer some answers to these questions, they are not meant to be taken as truths. Blind acceptance of any so-called "truth" would in fact hinder one's development of insight. The "answers" provided here function merely as guidelines based on the experiences of the masters of the past. It is the responsibility of the meditators to find their own answers and to thus make the practice relevant to their own experience.

*Start as usual by sitting in a comfortable position and **taking refuge**. Then generate the sublime motivation of **bodhicitta** (recite three times):*

In order to liberate all beings from the ocean of samsara I must attain the state of perfect and complete enlightenment. For that purpose I now engage in the following practice.

Then rest the mind for a while on the sensation of the breath streaming in and out of the nose. When the mind is calm and stable start with the training in vipashyana.

To generate enthusiasm for the practice contemplate the following:

The innate essence of my mind is naturally luminous and has never been tainted by conceptual elaborations. This nature of mind is luminosity and emptiness in undifferentiable union. Not realizing this, I have been clinging to dualistic appearances and to the self as truly existent. This has caused me to roam ceaselessly in this endless ocean of samsara.

Now, however, I will put into practice my teacher's instructions until I have mastered the unfathomable mystery of the profound mind, the essence of the eighty-four thousand teachings of the buddhas of the three times.

I will be mindful and exert myself not to be overpowered again by the delusional belief in the substantial existence of anything.

1. Analyzing the nature of the self of the individual

What is the *self* really? What is this "I"? Who, in reality, is this person, this substantially existing individual I assume to be? Is it my name, my body, or my mind?

My *name*, being merely a conventional label, is clearly not the self.

Is the *body* the self? If it were, then the self would be multiple, since this body is an aggregation composed of many distinct parts, such as the inner organs, the bones, the skin, and so forth. The self, however, is assumed to be one singular entity. It is therefore not identical with the body. From the top of my head down to the soles of my feet, I cannot locate the self, either inside or outside the body, can I?

Could it be the *mind* then? The past mind has ceased and the future mind has not yet come to be. The present mind consists of nothing but ever-changing mental events, arising and ceasing moment by moment. The self understood to be the mind is therefore just a label imputed to the continuity of mind constructed on the basis of past, present, and future mental events.

For these reasons, that which I call "self" is only a projection of my delusion, a mere label imputed on the collection of body and mind.

2.   Recognizing the nature of appearances

The appearances of outer phenomena, such as trees, houses, the people I see, and even the sensation of my breath—in brief, everything I objectify, all these appearances are not produced accidentally, nor are they created by an almighty god or by the interaction of outer forces of nature. They also do not arise without a cause. These appearances are produced by my own delusion, conditioned by the latent tendencies present in my mind.

When I look at a glass of "water," for instance, I see "drinking water." This very water, however, may also be perceived as a habitat by the small creatures living in it. Different beings have different perceptions of the same object, corresponding to their own respective conditioning. Is what I label "water" *really* water, or is it that only for me? If so, what is its true nature?

What I perceive as "outer, real objects" are, therefore, like the appearances in a dream, and the mind which apprehends these objects is like the dreaming mind. Therefore, all phenomena, which consist of these dualistic appearances of subject and object, are but delusions and deceptions, mere projections of the mind with no reality of their own.

Contemplate the meaning of this and repeat this process until you have a strong, unshakable understanding of the lack of true existence of dualistic perceptions.

3.   Looking at the mind itself and resting in nonconceptual awareness

Now look at the present moment basic awareness, free from the veil of subject and object. Look nakedly at the natural radiance of this awareness over an extended period of time. When you experience this awareness as crisp clarity and vividness, examine it in the following manner.

Firstly, consider the origin of this awareness: where does it come from, what is its cause? Since one cannot find a cause for its initial arising, it is pristine emptiness in that it is unborn.

Then consider the essence of awareness: where does it reside at this very moment? It is neither inside the body, nor outside it, nor in between the two. It has neither color nor form. No matter how long one searches, it cannot be found. Therefore, it is pristine lucidity in that it is nonabiding.

Finally consider: where does it cease? Since this present moment awareness does not cease anywhere when giving rise to the next moment resultant awareness, it is serene bliss in that it is nonceasing.

Thus, being devoid of cause, essence, and result, the fundamental nature of mind is utterly bare in that it is emptiness, not existing in any way whatsoever.

The natural expression of the clarity of the mind which experiences this emptiness is vibrant lucidity in that it is a cognitive experience which does not cease anywhere.

This very lucidity cannot be found to exist in any way whatsoever. While being empty, clear awareness does not cease. Therefore, with complete wakefulness, settle vividly and nakedly in its natural state devoid of clinging to either clarity or emptiness, impartial in that it is free from conceptual extremes, and beyond the intellect in that it is inexpressible.

Without clinging even to the concept of mere inexpressibility, settle in this state of vast spaciousness. If a thought arises, do not let it develop into a stream of thoughts, but completely cut it and again place the mind in the state of nongrasping.

In the beginning of this process tightly focus the mind to settle in this state; then let the mind relax to rest in this state; and finally, settle in the state free of expectation and apprehension.

In brief, remain without effort in this state which is undistracted from this awareness devoid of clinging to either clarity or emptiness. Settle in this state in which there is nothing whatsoever to cultivate. Practice in this way intensely, but for short periods, again and again. Do not overdo it. Continue the meditation session as long as the quality of the practice is still good, taking care to end it before negative feelings arise.

At the end of the meditation session, before arising from the posture of meditation, recite:

> The true nature of all things is free from conceptual extremes, it is inexpressible and beyond the intellect. It has no basis, is devoid of roots, and is like space. Not realizing this, all these sentient beings who have been my mother are bound with the tight fetters of grasping to an "I" and to the duality of subject and object. They are completely enmeshed in a world of appearances rooted in their confusion. I feel such pity for them. For their sake, I will do whatever it takes to attain the state of complete buddhahood, the realization of mind's true nature, utterly free from conceptual extremes.

*Then **dedicate** the merit of this practice to all sentient beings:*

> By this merit may I attain omniscience.
> Defeating the foe, the harmful afflictions,
> May I liberate beings from the ocean of samsara,
> Disturbed by the waves of birth, old age, sickness,
> and death.

> Just like the heroic Manjushri,
> Who knows things just as they are,
> And like Samantabhadra too,
> May I follow them all in the ways they have trained,
> And completely dedicate all these virtues.

Selected bibliography

Chogye Trichen Rinpoche. *Parting from the Four Attachments: Jetsun Drakpa Gyaltsen's Song of Experience on Mind Training and the View.* Ithaca, N.Y.: Snow Lion Publications, 2003.

Deshung Rinpoche. *The Three Levels of Spiritual Perception: An Oral Commentary on* The Three Visions (Snang gsum) *of Ngorchen Konchog Lhundrub.* 2nd ed. Boston: Wisdom Publications, 2003.

Jamgön Kongtrül. *The Treasury of Knowledge, Book 5: Buddhist Ethics.* Ithaca, N.Y.: Snow Lion Publications, 2003.

Khenchen Appey Rinpoche. *Teachings on Sakya Pandita's* Clarifying the Sage's Intent. 2nd rev. ed. Kathmandu: Vajra Publications, 2008.

Khenchen Appey Rinpoche. *Cultivating a Heart of Wisdom: Oral Instructions on the Mind Training in Seven Points.* Kathmandu: Vajra Books, 2014.

Khenpo Jamyang Tenzin. *The Meditator's Nest: Building a Spiritual Practice.* Kathmandu: International Buddhist Academy, 2016.

Kunzang Pelden. *The Nectar of Manjushri's Speech: A Detailed Commentary on Shantideva's* Way of the Bodhisattva. Translated by the Padmakara Translation Group. Boston: Shambhala, 2010.

Ngorchen Konchog Lhundrub. *The Three Visions: Fundamental Teachings of the Sakya Lineage of Tibetan Buddhism.* 2nd ed. Ithaca, N.Y.: Snow Lion Publications, 2002.

Pearcey, Adam. *A Compendium of Quotations.* Sixth Edition. Lotsawa School, 2008.

Shāntideva. *The Way of the Bodhisattva: A Translation of the* Bodhicharyāvatāra. Translated by the Padmakara Translation Group. Rev. ed. Boston: Shambhala, 2006.

*By the merit of this work
may all beings attain perfect awakening.*

The **Chödung Karmo Translation Group** (CKTG) was founded in 2010 at the **International Buddhist Academy** (IBA) in Kathmandu, Nepal, to help fulfill the late Khenchen Appey Rinpoche's vision for the preservation and transmission of the Buddha Dharma, specializing in translating works of masters from the Sakya tradition.

The main aims of IBA are to promote the study and practice of the Buddha's teachings by offering in-depth courses in English on Buddhist thought and meditation retreats, to digitize and publish Tibetan Dharma texts, and to offer language and leadership training to young Tibetan monks of the Sakya tradition.

Please visit our websites for more information:

www.chodungkarmo.org
www.internationalbuddhistacademy.org